Book 1

Understanding and Making Peace With Your Darker Side

By

Kelly Wallace

Professional Psychic Counselor

DrKellyPsychic.com[1]

---

1. http://DrKellyPsychic.com/

© 2020 All Rights Reserved

Intuitive Living Publishing

Table of Contents

Books by Kelly Wallace 1

About Kelly Wallace 4

What This Book Covers 5

Introduction 7

Part One | - Understanding Your Shadow - 9

The Shadow-Self 10

Your Shadow Is Real 13

How Your Shadow Was Created 16

You're Always Being Tested 18

Your Shadow Makes Bad Choices 21

The Mirror Effect 24

Facing Your Shadow 26

The Gift of The Shadow 28

Detoxing Your Soul 30

Part Two | - Shadow Work Exercises - 33

First Steps In Shadow Work 34

Going In Deeper 36

Giving Your Shadow A Voice 46

Dissolving Shadow-Projections.. 50

Letting Go Of Resistance 53

Shadows In Your Relationships 57

Sorting Through Your Stuff 60

Releasing Shadows Of The Past 63

Contact Me/Book A Reading 66

Books by Kelly Wallace

10 Minutes A Day to A Powerful New Life

Become Your Higher Self – Using Spiritual Energy to Transform Your Life

Breaking The Worry Habit – Stop Your Anxious Thoughts And Start Living!

Chakras – Heal, Clear, And Strengthen Your Energy Centers

Clear Your Karma – The Healing Power of Your Past Lives

Contacting Your Spirit Guides – Meeting and Working with Your Invisible Helpers

Creating A Charmed Life – Enchantments to Attract, Repel, Cleanse & Heal

Dream Work – Using The Wisdom Of Your Sleeping Mind To Change Your Waking Life

Energy Work – Heal, Cleanse, and Strengthen Your Aura

Everyday Miracles – Powerful Steps to Wonderful Experiences

Finding Your Life Purpose – Uncover Your Soul's True Goals

Healing the Child Within – Rewrite Your Early Childhood Life Script

How to Cure Candida – Yeast Infection Symptoms, Causes, Diet & Natural Remedies

Intuitive Living – Developing Your Psychic Gifts

Intuitive Tarot – Learn the Tarot Instantly

Is He The One? Finding And Keeping Your Soulmate

Master the Art of Picking Up Women

Master the Art of Dating Women

Master the Art of Sex and Seduction

No-Sweat Homeschooling – The Cheap, Free, and Low-Stress Way to Teach Your Kids

Psychic Vampires – Protect and Heal Yourself from Energy Predators

Reprogram Your Subconscious – Use The Power Of Your Mind

Shadow Work Book 1 – Understanding And Making Peace With Your Darker Side

Shadow Work Book 2 – Facing and Embracing the Dark Side of Your Soul

Spirit Guides And Healing Energy – Worth Your Guides, Aura, and Chakras

Spiritual Alchemy – Transform Your Life and Everyone In It

The Art Of Happiness – Living A Life Of Peace And Simplicity

The Love You Deserve – Release Toxic Relationships and Attract Your Soulmate

The Mended Soul – Healing Your Mind, Body, & Spirit From Anxiety & Depression

The Overwhelmed Empath – A Guide For Sensitive Souls

The Power of Pets – How to Psychically Communicate with Your Pet

Transforming Your Money Mindset – From Broke To Abundance

True Wealth – Reprogram Your Subconscious for Financial Success

Upgrade Your Life – Small Changes, Easy Actions, Big Success

Working With Your Angels – Learn To Contact Them and Recognize Their Guidance

About Kelly Wallace

Kelly is a bestselling spiritual and self-help author, former radio show host, and has been a professional psychic counselor for over twenty years. She can see, hear, sense, and feel information sent from Spirit, the Universe, and a client's Higher Self.

She offers professional psychic counseling, caring guidance, and solutions that work! More than just a typical psychic reading or counseling session, you will feel you've found a real friend during your time of need—whether you simply want answers and guidance to your current worries or concerns, or you're interested in learning more about your soulmate, spirit guides, angels, past lives, or anything else.

Contact her today for an in-depth and life-altering reading!

Website: DrKellyPsychic.com[1]

Email: Dr.Kelly.Psychic.Counselor@gmail.com

---

1. http://psychicreadingsbydrkelly.webs.com/

What This Book Covers

Introduction

Part One: Understanding Your Shadow

The Shadow-Self

Your Shadow Is Real

How Your Shadow Was Created

You're Always Being Tested

Your Shadow Makes Bad Choices

The Mirror Effect

Facing Your Shadow

The Gift Of The Shadow

Detoxing Your Soul

Part Two: Shadow Work Exercises

First Steps In Shadow Work

Going In Deeper

Giving Your Shadow A Voice

Dissolving Shadow Projections

6

Letting Go of Resistance

Shadows In Your Relationships

Sorting Through Your Stuff

Releasing Shadows Of The Past

Contact Me/Book A Reading

Introduction

We all have a darker side, even if we're not aware of it or don't want to believe it. When you ignore this shadow though it gets bigger and stronger, and eventually starts making all of your decisions for you. You might think that you're consciously directing your life, but you aren't. Not at all. In this book, *Shadow Work – Understanding And Making Peace With Your Darker Side*, I want to show you how you can work on healing your shadow-self rather than hiding from it.

Everyone is conflicted between who they truly are and who they want to be. We show the outside world one side of our personality, the light one, the acceptable one, or the one we believe we're supposed to put on display.

Inside ourselves, it's a different story. There's a constant struggle going on there because we believe life needs to be either/or. We're either good or bad, kind or rude, confident or uncertain, generous or greedy, and so on. The truth is, we're both sides of the coin. One can't exist within you without the other existing as well.

Believing that your shadow self isn't real is what's keeping you from making better choices and living the life you desire and deserve. Why? Because, all of your power has been handed over to your shadow and it's the one in charge at the moment.

Since childhood, you've been taught to hide this part of yourself. Now, if you so much as sense a bad thought or feeling trying to surface, you either act on it without thinking or shove it back down inside and pray that it doesn't show itself again. But it will, again and again.

Your shadow isn't a bad thing, though we believe these parts of us are somehow unacceptable. Soon, it becomes our enemy. A monster living within us that we fear yet can never escape from. The more you run, the stronger it gets, and the more regret, pain, and suffering you'll face.

To change all of that, you need to discover why your shadow took up residence in the first place and all of the experiences that have added to its strength over the years. Once you do, you can then work on resolving them. Soon, you'll be living the life you were meant to live by embracing those darker parts and making your shadow work with you rather than against you.

Part One
- Understanding Your Shadow -

The Shadow-Self

To put it briefly, in Jungian psychology, the shadow is either an unconscious feature of the personality that the conscious ego doesn't identify in itself or the whole of the unconscious. It's everything we're not fully aware of; the unknown, dark side of ourselves.

Since the shadow is instinctive and irrational, it often projects onto others what we unconsciously view as faults within ourselves. Nobody likes to think badly of themselves so we keep these parts of our personality hidden, believing it's "them" and not "us". But, the longer we ignore or deny this part of ourselves, the more we give it the power to create what we dislike or fear most.

This isn't a psychology book though since my profession is in dealing with spiritual issues. I want to teach you how to recognize, understand, and finally make peace with your shadow-self through simple exercises and activities. Does that mean you should destroy that part of yourself? Get rid of those dark parts that have caused you so much trouble and frustration? No.

Getting rid of your shadow would be like cutting yourself in half. You need both to have balance and to be whole. We're merely going to shine light into those dark places so you can see them more clearly rather than being blind to them. You'll make peace with these issues and learn to use them to your advantage. But, it won't happen overnight. Instead, it will be like peeling back layer after layer of an enormous onion.

When I refer to your dark side or shadow-self, I'm referring to the anger, fear, sadness, rejection, shame, denial, and embarrassment that we all stuff deep inside. Why do we do this? Because, we're taught from a young age that these feelings aren't acceptable, so we go through life pasting on a false front and adding more layers to the shadow within.

Whether you've struggled with money, weight, love, or just about anything else, you can bet that your shadow-self needs to be faced at long last and worked on. Once you do, you should notice your life changing in both small and dramatic ways. You'll attract more positive people and better opportunities. Life will be happier, smoother, and far more abundant.

In my years of practice, I've seen clients go from loveless or abusive relationships to stable, soulmate marriages. People who have declared bankruptcy and are on the verge of homelessness now having a steady paycheck and positive financial futures. Those who have gone from being severely overweight and riddled with pain, to reaching their goal weight and feeling healthier and more energetic than they had in decades.

I'll be honest though, shadow work isn't for the faint of heart or those who give up easily. After all, you're going to be facing some scary, negative, and unflattering things that have been buried inside you for some time. These deep-seated traits are usually formed in early childhood, then compounded on over time.

You can't deny the existence of your shadow any longer. I can guarantee that if you've been repeating the same patterns and attracting the same type of people and events in your life, no matter how hard you've tried to make changes, your shadow-self is the one in charge. Let's change all that. Let's get to work on creating the type of life you've always wanted!

Your Shadow Is Real

Your shadow-self isn't like a true shadow, and it's not your enemy either. Instead, it's simply a part of you, part of your soul and mental makeup. It's a collection of all the thoughts and feelings you've been denying or suppressing since you first came into this world. Yes, your shadow is born the moment you're born! How is it created though?

- Have you ever been angry, but stuffed it down instead? Well, that becomes part of your shadow-self.

- Have you ever felt victimized but said nothing and did nothing because feeling sorry for yourself just isn't accepted? That, too, becomes part of your shadow-self.

- If you've felt hurt, worried, or afraid and wanted to cry but didn't. Every time you stuff down any so-called negative emotion, it's all saved and never goes away, becoming part of your shadow.

But is it only negative feelings that end up there? Not at all. Positive emotions are stored there as well because sometimes we're just not willing to accept things like happiness, love, caring, success, and hope. For some of us, it's a lot easier to accept pain and unhappiness than it is to embrace anything good, especially if you're life has been particularly difficult from a young age.

We get used to what we know, and if all we know is misery then this is what we'll accept. Happiness and love? That's far too scary.

It's better to ignore it and hide it away in those dark recesses of the soul, never to be looked at again. And yet all of it lingers there, growing each day. Knowing this, can you imagine how big your shadow has become after all these years?

People with the biggest shadows usually walk around asleep, unaware, and numb to everything because facing the good, the bad, and the ugly seems too overwhelming. I've been there myself. Just going through the motions of life, never feeling much, and just accepting the way things are since "this is how it's always been".

I view my shadow almost like a second yet different "me". This other me isn't an enemy. In fact, she's just been misunderstood. She's always wanted to be honest and true to herself, yet I didn't let her. With a dysfunctional upbringing and following the rules of polite society I silenced her and let my ego take over. My ego, that conscious part of myself, always acts the same with very little emotional upheaval. I imagine it as a smooth, never-ending road.

My shadow-self? If I imagined her I'd sometimes see her as huge, angry, and loud. Yet other times she'd be filled with light, wisdom, and love. She's as honest as honest can be—unlike my ego. But I hated that roller coaster ride of emotions so I'd stay on that never-ending smooth highway most of the time. Boring, right? But safe and predictable.

With my shadow-self, I never know what she'll present me with. And yet, I often seek her out. I'll spend time in thought, meditation, or journaling, asking her questions and listening to her. Sometimes she's so upset that I want to stop what I'm doing and race back to the light, but I know that this is where I'll learn the most. Where all true healing takes place.

If we aren't listening to our authentic selves, how can we ever hope to have the success, love, and happiness we've craved for so long? We can't. Any positive you find would be short-lived and/or incredibly superficial because you haven't worked on those dark corners of your mind and soul.

Take a look at the people around you. Are they angry? Do they gossip and complain? Are they always down on their luck and can never accomplish anything they pursue? Are there people who get on your nerves, push your buttons, and annoy the hell out of you? Take a look around to see who or what gets your attention or gets on your nerves. Guess what? That's your shadow making itself known. Like attracts like. And, as much as we want to deny it, we truly are who and what we are deep inside. Anything that strikes an emotional chord in you is a reflection of your shadow.

Your shadow isn't trying to torture you though. Instead, it's bringing people and events into your life that are a mirror of what you're denying and ignoring. It wants you to work through these issues so that both your light and dark parts can live in harmony.

How Your Shadow Was Created

We learn from an early age that certain qualities and personality traits aren't acceptable in society and within our family. If we display any of these emotions that are considered negative our parents, teachers, other adults in our lives, and our peers will criticize, reject, or shun us. When this happens our self-esteem plummets so we learn to avoid doing or saying anything that could cause people to look down on us or exclude us.

As a child, the messages we constantly hear are to be this way, not that way, and act this way, not that way. Every family is different and parents have different expectations for their children. Maybe in your family "acting like a lady" was important so any time you played rough, got dirty, or yelled you would get in trouble. Or, perhaps your father wanted you to be "a real man" so crying, being sensitive, or anything else that he might label as weak or feminine was criticized. Over time, all of these so-called negative personality traits were sent right into the basement—your shadow-self.

Since we learn what's acceptable and what isn't we eventually start doing this to ourselves. Anything that doesn't conform to your own idea of a positive self-image is banished and becomes part of the shadow. I've seen creative people give up their artistic dreams because they didn't fit in with their competitive, business-driven friends. I've also seen people squash down their happy, silly side so they'd fit in with their more serious and sophisticated friends.

If that isn't bad enough, as human beings we all want to be valued, liked, loved, and accepted. So what do we do to secure those very things? We hide any emotions or behaviors that we feel others will find objectionable or undesirable, and all of that becomes part of the shadow as well.

Soon, all of these "forbidden" feelings and behaviors are buried so deeply we aren't even aware that they exist at all. But, they do exist and they'll eventually rise up.

You're Always Being Tested

Everyone on this Earth—past, present, and future—has a shadow that started taking shape in infancy. As the years passed we tucked more and more things away so we could create what we felt was a positive self-image and fit in with those around us.

Your shadow never goes away though, even if you're completely unaware that it exists. There will always be times when that darker side pops up, forcing you to face it, work through it, and ultimately accept that part of yourself. How does your shadow test you?

Have you ever met someone you really disliked? Do you know someone who has a personality trait that irritates you? Have you ever been overwhelmed by shame, envy, or anger? If so, that's part of your shadow rising to the surface, trying to get your attention. Whenever you have a strong, unreasonable reaction or aversion to what you perceive as negative qualities in someone else ... that's your very own shadow.

Let me use myself as an example. I have a friend who gets her nails and hair done every week, orders food delivery almost daily, has an expensive car, and designer shoes. She can't afford any of this and is always living paycheck-to-paycheck, if that. Many times her bank account has had a negative balance and all of her credit cards are maxed out.

Just seeing how she is with her finances stresses me out and I feel critical of her need to always indulge herself. She's forever saying that she "deserves this", "has deprived herself too long", "is stressed and needs this or that to feel better", and so on. The way she uses her money really leaves me speechless.

But why should her frivolous spending bother me so much? If I look deep inside I can recognize that my critical judgment and intolerance about her comes from my own shadow. Knowing that this is what's happening, I can admit to myself that I'm such a frugal person, having come from poverty, that I often deny myself even the smallest treat. All of this self-denial has made me feel angry and deprived at times. Do I like feeling this way? Not at all, but I can recognize *why* I have this automatic reaction and then work through it.

Why do we fight against these feelings though and why do we despise in others the very things that are buried in our shadow? Because, we see ourselves the way we'd like to be and we want others to see us this way as well. It's only a small part of our true selves though. The outside that we show others and believe is the real us is not all that we are. We're so much more.

Learning to embrace your dark side can help you open up and become who you truly are—all facets of you. Being this open and this aware is so incredibly healing and will help you to be a whole person and improve your mood, your life, and your relationships because you'll be your true self—warts and all.

This self-awareness is such a big part of personal growth and it all starts with doing shadow work. This involves making friends and making peace with your darker side and embracing your whole self, not just the more acceptable, flattering parts of you. The more you accept your shadow, the less judgmental and more tolerant you'll become.

Another positive thing that comes with acknowledging your shadow side is that you can then choose how and when to express these "dark" tendencies. Rather than just reacting to them or stuffing them down when they make themselves known, you can choose to cry, be angry, envious, indulge yourself, or any other emotions you've suppressed for so long. But, you can do so in a more responsible way.

Your Shadow Makes Bad Choices

I'm sure you can look back on various decisions you've made in life that you later regretted. I've done that myself more times than I can count. Sometimes we make these decisions because we're in a vulnerable state: you just got out of a long-term relationship, someone close to you passed away, you lost your job, your car needs expensive repairs, etc.

When something traumatic happens it tends to knock us off balance. The change might be necessary or forced upon us, but one thing humans cling to is trying to hold on to what we know. But when we're in the middle of a crisis, whatever it is, it's hard to think clearly. So, when a decision needs to be made but your mind isn't where you want it to be you can often end up making one of the worst decisions of your life. This is usually because the shadow-self has taken over and made the decision for you.

Since your shadow has been locked away and ignored for so long it's far less mature than you currently are and it will typically make bad decisions. There are times when we're so overwhelmed that the logical, conscious mind can't decide so the shadow does. The problem is, it's usually something that's immature, though at the moment it's our only coping mechanism. While you've been spending year after year maturing and growing, your shadow-self has stayed the same.

Whether you stuffed down an emotion at five years old, fifteen, twenty, or any other age, that's the logic that comes with it. You go right back to being a child, or a teenager, or young adult when you first had that experience then buried it. So, the way you cope with it will be the same and it won't work since you're different now and the situation is obviously different too. As you can imagine, this just makes everything worse.

This isn't always a negative thing though. I feel it's important to face your shadow and work through the lessons it brings. That's when true growth takes place.

Years ago I was getting out of an abusive marriage. Since I was raised in an abusive household as a child, my first instinct was to run. I was overwhelmed and couldn't think straight while going through this breakup. So, what happened? My shadow-self rose up and took over ... and I ran. I packed up my kids and moved across the country from one coast to the other. After the dust settled, so to speak, I asked myself, "What the hell am I doing here?" Yes, it gave me some distance from my ex, but life was very difficult in other ways.

But you know what? All in all, it was a good experience that allowed me to work through my child-self and all of those life scripts that had been sent down into my shadow. So, although I would have liked life to be easier, that part of me chose a difficult route, but I've grown so much because of it. Our shadow shows us what we need to work on and overcome so we can become whole and integrated rather than fragmented.

This is why I often see bad decisions and difficult decisions as a blessing. They help us to face what we need to, grow where needed, and let go of what no longer serves us. When we do this, being able to identify when the shadow-self is trying to take over, we can learn from it and remove those barriers then make better decisions in the future.

The Mirror Effect

Your shadow will project onto others what you deny in yourself. If we judge, complain, criticize, blame, or pick others apart, that's your shadow making its appearance. These are a mirror of the things within ourselves that we try to hide away from the world. It's as if we're trying to convince ourselves, "Oh! That person's behavior is so terrible. I would never do that!"

In reality, these very things exist inside of you but you've done a really good job at hiding them. You've spent so many years covering up everything you're ashamed of and it started in early childhood. The first time someone hurt you, belittled you, or made you feel ashamed, you automatically stuffed it into your shadow. You didn't have to think about it, it just happened.

As the years went on you added more and more to this darker part of yourself. You were rejected? Angry? Embarrassed? Criticized? Emotionally wounded? Down it all went into that deep well. The older you got, the harder you worked at repressing these things you perceived as inadequacies because they made you feel insecure. We all do our best to keep our repressed fears hidden from the world because we're ashamed of those parts of ourselves.

Healing your shadow and becoming comfortable with it will take time and work, but it's necessary if you want to be at peace and be whole. Just admitting that you have a shadow side is the first step to healing. In a bit, we'll cover other steps so you can work with this hidden part of yourself.

Facing Your Shadow

We spend so much of life hiding our fears, running from our heartaches, and squashing down our anger, shame, and pain. In fact, we get so used to doing this that it becomes automatic. All of this denial creates huge roadblocks and repeated patterns.

There's a saying, "If you don't work it out, you'll act it out". So, all that stuff you've been burying doesn't stay buried. It's all there, in your subconscious, and will come to the surface again and again until you admit your truth. It takes a lot of courage to face your shadow, but imagine the possibilities once you do! You'll be able to find all the peace, happiness, and success you've been looking for but could never find.

Most people never face their darker side though. They've either convinced themselves it doesn't really exist or believe they can keep hiding from it. I can guarantee though, when you least expect it, when your defenses are down, or when life hits you with an unwelcome surprise, it's going to leak out.

Typically, your shadow will sabotage you by taking the form of doubt, fear, distraction, or procrastination any time you try to take a step up in life. Our shadow also keeps us stuck in unhealthy relationships and dead-end jobs, addictions, and a long list of negative behaviors.

When your shadow springs to the surface your emotions will always be out of proportion to the situation. You'll feel intense rage, sadness, shame, hurt, or worry that's so much bigger than the actual event you're currently facing. These explosive emotions aren't necessarily bad, they're just trying to get your attention and let you know that there are deeper issues to be worked on.

If we're honest with ourselves we'll admit that it's exhausting to keep denying and hiding our shadows. If we never face them, not only will we continually sabotage our best efforts, but over the years, those toxic emotions can show up as physical pain and disease.

The next time your shadow comes to the surface, rather than ignoring it or pushing it back down, use it as a chance to resolve long-ignored emotions and experiences. Once you get to the root cause and face it head-on you'll begin to heal. Your energy will be free, allowing you to finally live life as your authentic self.

The Gift of The Shadow

So far, everything we've been talking about that relates to the shadow has seemed negative, but in reality, it's truly a gift. Your shadow was formed many years ago as a way to cope with stress and to protect you.

For example, if you were criticized as a child by someone you trusted and looked up to, such as a parent or teacher, you might have internally translated that into feelings of shame, guilt, or self-doubt. This became part of your shadow. Since then, you could have reacted to criticism either as never trying at all (so you avoid criticism altogether), or becoming angry (so people don't see that you truly feel vulnerable). Although your shadow really does have your best interest at heart, you've outgrown that type of "protection" and no longer need it.

Yes, there are times when being sad, angry, or any other seemingly negative emotion, is called for. Your shadow side just doesn't know how or when to use it and will often blow things out of proportion and explode into rage or tears. Or, even worse, you might not express those feelings at all and hold it all inside where it just festers and grows even bigger and stronger.

Everything we consider to be awful feelings and behaviors always have a positive intention—even if it doesn't work out that way. Rather than seeing this shadow side of yourself as embarrassing or frustrating, ask yourself how those emotional reactions protect you.

For instance, anger is very often a cover for other emotions we either haven't expressed or are afraid to express. It's also a way to let us know when someone has crossed the line and we need to stand up for ourselves or set boundaries.

It's easy to think that we'll finally find peace, joy, and the freedom we've been seeking by working on our outer life. You convince yourself that you'll be happier if you get a better job, lose weight, make more friends, move to a better home, buy a newer car, etc.

But everything you've been looking for is way down in the deepest, darkest part of yourself. Finding the courage to ask yourself those hard questions and seeing what comes up is what will lead you to the life you've always imagined having.

Where have you been hurt in life or held back? Just acknowledging this can often start to release those shadows. Remind yourself that you're an adult now and no longer a helpless child or victim. Be compassionate with your shadow-self though because it originated out of hurt.

Detoxing Your Soul

It's common to focus on detoxing your body. Whether you do a juice cleanse, fasting, clean eating, or something else. Nobody talks about detoxing the soul though. But if you think about it, everything you've been through is stored inside your soul. All of this "stuff" is what moves you forward in life or holds you back.

There's hardly a person on this Earth that isn't unconsciously holding themselves back or sabotaging themselves in some way. It's all because of the things taking up space in your soul and creating those shadows you've tried to avoid looking at all these years.

In truth, all of the things piled up in your shadow are really just your fears. And they'll stay there, clinging to you, growing bigger and stronger, until you heal and release them. One of our biggest tasks in life is identifying and releasing the toxic issues that have been standing in our way. Until you do, your shadow-self is going to have you repeating negative patterns until you finally get the message and face it all head-on.

The first step to this emotional and spiritual cleanse is to no longer deny these issues and traumas that have wounded you. Now, there's a difference between just saying, "Yeah, my dad had an anger problem"—or whatever is in your past—and really acknowledging the harm it did to you, allowing it to surface, and feeling it. This is where most people run and hide, squashing down that shadow yet again.

It's difficult to face your inner demons, those wounded and scarred parts of yourself. Nobody likes feeling weak or like a bad person, so it's easier to live in a state of denial. However, as the years roll by that shadow will become more insistent, life will be more challenging and disappointing.

Also, you'll project those things onto others more and more until you finally get the message and work on healing yourself. The alternative is to continue denying it and leaving this world with a shadow larger than your soul.

Maybe you don't feel up to working on those issues at the moment. That's perfectly okay, but know that all of that stuff isn't just going to disappear. Sure, the shadow might go into hibernation for a short time, but it will rise up again in the near future and you'll have yet another opportunity to work through things. That's why we repeat patterns in life. We've been in denial but that part of your soul wants you to pay attention and become whole, so here comes that lesson again.

Once you acknowledge the issue(s) you can then work on healing—and this is where things get really difficult. You've become an expert at pretending the pain isn't there, have learned to live with it, and probably assumed that it was all in the past. That's not how it works though.

That pain and those fears offer a lot of information about why it keeps showing up in your life. Yes, whatever happened to you is now in the past. Back then you were a victim and you learned these negative ways of being from someone else. Now it's your own responsibility to overcome it.

After you've gone through the healing process you can then work on releasing the issue(s) altogether. That isn't the end of it though. You'll then need to be vigilant about not falling back into those old patterns. It will take time to become comfortable without that old program always running in the background of your mind.

Human beings thrive on habit and your mind is going to do anything it can to get you to go back to that comfort zone you knew so well. Yes, even though those old patterns were toxic, you got used to them. When you feel that shadow part rising to the surface remind yourself that you're okay, there's nothing to fear, and you can move forward with confidence and courage.

Shadow work is so important in detoxing your soul, though it takes time and patience. If you never work on these issues and keep them buried inside they'll eventually take over every part of your life and you'll never be free.

Part Two
- Shadow Work Exercises -

First Steps In Shadow Work

Think of your conscious and unconscious like a deck of cards. Rather than having all the red cards (your ego) trying to control your life or the black cards (your shadow) truly being the one guiding your every step, you shuffle the cards again and again until they're well mixed. This way life flows so much better and easier and you take each emotion as it comes, acknowledging it and working through it.

Let's look at some first steps to working with your shadow:

1. Allow yourself to feel your feelings and think your thoughts. Don't dismiss them or squash them down. If you feel an automatic reaction then this is especially important. This is your shadow-self sending you a message that it's something you need to work on.

2. Assure yourself that you can handle this. No matter how scared or sad or angry you feel, remind yourself that this is only pain and you're never given more than you can handle. Breathe through it. Accept it. Embrace the fact that these feelings are part of you, not something you should deny.

3. Your shadow will make itself known in the world around you. Whether it's someone who frustrates you, an angry person in the checkout line behind you, or an article you read that won't leave your mind. These are your shadow parts coming out. Recognizing this fact is important.

Ignoring these dark parts of you will only add to your misery and disappointment. The fact is, it will not go away until you acknowledge it and work through it.

Going In Deeper

It's easy to believe that we're consciously in control of our lives, our emotions, and our actions. The truth is, your shadow is the one guiding you most of the time, making you live and react in ways that frustrate or even shock you.

I'm sure you can look back on your past and recall some times when you made a decision or reacted to a situation and later said to yourself, "Why did I do that!" We convince ourselves that we've never acted that way before, but if you're completely honest you'll see that you *have* reacted that way many times. Your shadow will keep repeating the same things over and over until you finally face it. Sure, maybe the circumstances are a bit different each time, but the outcome always ends up being the same.

For instance, every relationship I had gotten into always ended up the same: dysfunctional and eventually ended, and usually on bad terms. No matter how supposedly conscious I tried to be of this, no matter how different each guy seemed from the last, the end result was the same.

Not until I realized that my shadow was the one choosing these men, rather than my conscious self, was I able to make positive changes. It didn't happen overnight though. The shadow likes routine and when you attempt to make any changes it will dig in its heels, trying to prevent you from doing things differently from what's been programmed into it for so long.

There are several ways to bring your shadow out into the open and begin working with it so it will no longer control you.

Shadow Work Exercises:

1. Acknowledge it

Your shadow is part of you so there's no reason to be afraid of it, and ignoring it is the worst thing you can do. That just means it will have control over your entire life for the rest of your life. Although you might not want to believe it, you're the one that created it. Yes, the traumas and other difficult times we go through in life are where it originated, but you're the one who keeps it growing.

2. You're In Control

You're always in control of your emotional reactions—if you catch them in time—but the shadow is almost always faster than you are. Why? Because that programming runs deep and you don't even need to think about it. It's an automatic reaction when you're faced with something that triggers that part of you. Yes, you can change all that, but being conscious of your emotional reactions takes a few steps:

- You need to first catch yourself when you notice that dark part of you springing to the surface.

- You need to consciously choose how you'd prefer to react to the moment.

- You then need to act on this wiser decision.

Your shadow doesn't need to do any of this. It's as easy as flipping a switch. This is why shadow work takes time, patience, and dedication. Always remind yourself that *you are in control*.

3. Take Its Energy Away

Your shadow absolutely loves living in the past. This is where it got its energy to begin with, and every time you react to something as you did in the past, you're just feeding it more fuel. Not until you start doing things differently when it comes to emotionally charged situations will your shadow stop playing that same well-worn reaction again and again.

You can't blame your shadow too much though. After all, it truly believes it's helping you. You developed those automatic reactions long ago to help you deal with some trauma you went through, but the shadow never matures. Instead, it stays at the same mental stage as you were when you experienced that negative episode the first time. Ever since then it's been holding back your personal growth and ultimate happiness.

4. Let Go Of The Past

I know, if letting go of the past was that easy you wouldn't be dealing with your shadow. You can be 100% honest and acknowledge your trauma of the past, truly believe you've made peace with it, and then out of nowhere, it pops up again, sabotaging your best efforts.

What really helped me was to not actually look at the episode itself that caused the original trauma, but how it affected me and what my reaction was then. I can then see how I've reacted similarly throughout the years every time I'm faced with that emotional trigger. This allowed me to have compassion for the young person inside of me that was wounded so long ago rather than rehashing "what that person did to me".

This is how you truly heal from the past.

5. Be Patient

This is where most people fail to heal their shadow. We live in a world where we want instant gratification and quick results. Shadow work isn't quick and it's not always painless either, but it's necessary if you want a different kind of life. It's baby steps all the way. It's stripping away layer after layer of paint until you get to the wood beneath so you can actually see what's there. It's easy to feel exhausted and defeated, but you need to keep going.

6. Be Brave.

As you find some new insight, some other splinter of pain that's trying to control you, breathe through it, and let it know that you no longer need to react this way. You're different now. You aren't the same person who was hurt, embarrassed, neglected, or bullied that you were all those years ago so there's no need to keep using the same emotional tactics. After all, they haven't gotten you anywhere except feeling stuck and disappointed.

Be prepared for your shadow to put up a fight and just stay with these feelings. Be patient and loving with this part of yourself. Only when you stop fighting against it will you finally begin to heal.

7. Identify Your Triggers

Your shadow was programmed decades ago due to your emotional reactions to past experiences. Any trauma you faced in any form, especially as a child, created the very way you react to the same type of emotional issues today. Go back as far as you can when it comes to your triggers and I'm sure you'll see the patterns you've been repeating. Some of my triggers and how I used to handle them were:

- Getting into a seemingly good relationship, becoming afraid that I'd be abandoned, so I either sabotage things or simply choose Mr. Wrong each time already knowing things will fail. This way I'm not hurt or surprised when things don't work out. I already expected it.

- Being in crowded places, especially around strangers, has me going straight home where I feel safe, comfortable, and can decompress. Since my parents were avid party-goers when I was a child I was always in unfamiliar surroundings, around unfamiliar people. To this day I'm still an introvert at heart and don't mind this shadow side of myself. There are good aspects of our shadow too! It lets me know when I've been too overly stimulated, need to take a time out, and tend to some self-care.

- When faced with any type of life change, especially bigger ones, I cling hard to what I currently have and know—even if this change has the potential to be good for me. Having so much instability as a child, moving around all the time, and never knowing where we'd end up next showed me that "all change is bad change". That isn't true, but my shadow self didn't believe this.

- Avoiding confrontations at all costs, keeping the peace, not rocking the boat. Since my parents argued so much—screaming, throwing things, slamming doors—I learned from a young age to keep my mouth shut. Over time I realized that constructive confrontation and respectful conversations can help clear the air, heal things, and strengthen relationships.

What are your triggers? How do you typically handle them? How would you like to do things differently? How does your shadow actually help in some circumstances?

8. Be Aware Of Your Impulses

Most of the time we act without thinking, but when we do this we're just puppets to those pre-recorded programs deep inside. You act and react without even a conscious thought. Almost everything you do and every decision you make is automatic.

That's not necessarily bad if those unconscious actions aren't causing you any problems or holding you back. Things like driving to work, household chores, taking care of our kids and pets, all become routine and something we don't have to think about, we just do it.

When it comes to bigger things though, tell yourself that you won't make a decision without thinking about it first because acting on impulse can often lead to disappointment or disaster. I know this, so sometimes I'll pause only half a minute, or with something bigger I'll wait 24 hours or longer.

A perfect example of this is a client of mine who had gotten a decent amount of money from a settlement claim. As soon as that money hit her bank account she went and put a down payment on a new luxury car. She didn't need it, but she wanted it. She had been poor while growing up and her parents always drove around in an old, beat-up car.

She felt embarrassed when her mother would pull up in front of the school to drop her off and all her friends would see the "junk-mobile", as she called it. Her shadow-self wanted to avoid this embarrassment so she always strove to buy the newest car model and something fancy—even if she couldn't afford it.

This new car ended up being a nightmare for her. She couldn't keep up the payments and it was eventually repossessed. It was a tough lesson to learn, but since then she's been working really hard on those impulses and working through her feelings of shame from childhood.

Another client hated to be alone and would jump into one relationship after another. Her parents actually had a wonderful relationship, but her father passed away unexpectedly when she was 13 years old. Her mother was devastated, felt very lonely, depressed, and never pursued another relationship.

For my client, seeing how her mother was affected created an impulse in her that said, "Being alone is bad. It doesn't matter who I get together with, as long as I have someone." The very moment one relationship ended she was on dating sites looking for the next one.

With time, she realized why she was programmed to follow this dysfunctional path and has learned to be at peace with being single until the right person comes along.

Whether you're feeling worried, angry, afraid, nervous, or even overly excited, give yourself time to process your feelings. It will give your emotions a chance to calm down and cool off. By thinking things through you'll be able to make more rational choices. It's extremely rare when something needs an instantaneous decision, even if your shadow tries to convince you otherwise.

9. Let Go Of Regrets And Learn From Mistakes

It's so easy to beat ourselves up over mistakes from the past. We relive the episode, again and again, feeling the embarrassment, anger, and anxiety as if we'd just done that "dumb thing". The next time you feel yourself cringing or getting angry with yourself over something you did or didn't do in the past, allow yourself to reflect on this experience instead.

When you open up to this past episode the first thing you'll notice is your mind rebelling against the memory. Negative feelings will undoubtedly spring up and you'll either be consumed by them or try stuffing it all back down.

Instead, try to step outside of your emotions and ask yourself what you learned from this episode. Then be honest with yourself and see if you're still stuck in that negative pattern. Who or what is holding you back from releasing this?

Do your best to avoid feeling guilty or overwhelmed with regret. Tell yourself that you're trying to learn something, to grow, and move forward. Your shadow is showing you where you've been scarred in the past and have been hiding from it or reopening that wound again and again. Forgive yourself and remember the lesson you learned so you don't repeat it in the future.

It's perfectly okay, often healthy, and sometimes necessary to walk away from a situation that isn't allowing you to heal and grow. As an adult, you have free will to make the decisions that are best for you and your life. Sometimes you just need to find the courage to take the necessary actions without letting your shadow run the show.

10. Prepare For Your Future

Once you give your shadow-self a voice and start working through your issues you'll need to be aware of when your shadow tries to keep you tied to the past. The past is all your shadow knows and it can't see a better future for you.

Change terrifies your shadow because the way your shadow thinks is, "Something bad happened in the past and I've been protecting this person all this time. We're still alive, we're still getting through life. If there are changes, they could be worse than anything we've been through before and we might not survive!" Of course, this isn't true, but it's how that vulnerable part of yourself has been programmed.

Set aside some time when you're feeling optimistic and write down where you want to be in six months, then in a year, and then in five years. How would your life be different? How can you make these changes, slowly but surely, so this future becomes your reality? Then commit yourself to doing at least one thing each day that will get you closer to your goals.

11. Create A New You

What kind of person do you want to be? Do you want to be more confident, more outgoing, happier, healthier, or anything else? I'm sure you've heard the saying, "Fake it until you make it". This can help change your life as well. Start acting that way right now and each day. Pretend to be the way you want to be and eventually, this can become who you truly are. This really does work.

In the past, I've thought of people I've admired and wrote down some of their personality traits I wanted for myself. I wasn't trying to be this person specifically. I still wanted to be myself, but with these more confident traits. If I was faced with something that my shadow self would typically take over and run with, I'd pause and ask how this person I admire would handle it, and then I'd do it.

At first, it felt strange and completely fake because my darker side was trying to convince me that change was bad. But, I just kept pretending and soon I started feeling it emotionally. It didn't feel false anymore and that shadow side started accepting these good traits more and more.

Giving Your Shadow A Voice

This exercise is really good for getting in deep, finding out what you've been hiding or holding onto, and how your shadow has been controlling your thoughts and actions all this time. It can get intense and it isn't easy, but the things you'll learn about yourself can be eye-opening. Ultimately, these issues can be healed and released.

You'll need a mirror, full-length is best, but any mirror where you can see your face will work. You'll also need to set aside 10 minutes for this shadow work to be most effective, though, in the beginning, you might only be able to do it for a minute or two at most. What makes this exercise particularly difficult is that you'll be talking to yourself, looking into your own eyes, seeing the expressions on your face.

Since your eyes are a mirror of your soul, it's uncomfortable seeing all of those emotions welling up there and most people will end the exercise. Stick with this as long as you can though, adding on a few minutes each time you do it.

Don't be surprised if you cry. Just allow these tears to flow, knowing that pain is being released and your shadow is finally being heard. You'll know you've started the healing process when you can look into your eyes, interact with yourself about past issues, and feel a sense of calm. You might even smile.

I know you've spent a long, long time hiding from that wounded part of yourself. Now is the time to face those inner demons and discover that they really aren't out to harm or sabotage you. In time, you'll be working *with* your shadow rather than against it.

Before you start this exercise tell yourself that you aren't going to start judging yourself or say any demeaning or derogatory things. This will just get in the way of your healing. Promise yourself that you'll stay with this exercise as long as you can then try again tomorrow.

If you want to, you can set up your environment to be as relaxing as possible. When I do this exercise I usually light incense, a few candles, and have nature sounds or spiritual music playing softly in the background. This lets my mind know that what I'm doing is special and important.

Shadow Mirror Work Exercise:

1. Sit comfortably on the floor in front of the full-length mirror. Or, if you prefer, sit on your bed or in a chair and hold a hand mirror in front of your face. As you look into the mirror it's important to keep constant eye contact with yourself.

2. Now, say your full name and all the things that you are and why. Sounds easy, right?

I would just say, "I'm Kelly Margaret Wallace because that's what's on my birth certificate. I'm a mother because I had children, an author since I love writing, a psychic counselor because I have a passion to help others."

3. Go deeper now after you list these easy things that first come to your mind. Pause to reflect on who and what you are, and why. You should soon find that this becomes much more difficult as hidden things start coming to the surface.

I remember the first time I did this exercise I said, "I'm scared." After that came out of my mouth I just stopped, almost frozen, as I looked at myself. My breath caught in my chest and I could feel my heart start to beat faster. But, this is the good stuff you need to get to and uncover. This is your shadow finally having a voice. This is what's been controlling your life.

I'll admit, after I spoke those two words I was done for the day. I couldn't even verbalize *why* I was scared because it was like a backed-up train inside me. I felt those tears welling up inside me, all that old pain I'd shoved way down inside, and it was too much to handle.

I was gentle with myself though. I knew change wouldn't happen in just one session but I felt emotionally raw and needed a break. The very next day I tried it again and found that it was a little easier. With each passing day, I could feel myself opening up, being more honest, and braver.

Once you've sat with this for the full ten minutes you're going to feel spent and exhausted—mentally, physically, emotionally, and spiritually. If you can, do this exercise when you have a day or two off work. It's difficult, if not impossible, to do shadow work before or after a workday. You're going to need the energy for this exercise and time afterward to decompress and process what came up.

Don't hold back if you want to cry. Allow this release and remember that it's not only okay to cry, but it's incredibly healing and cleansing. You might feel angry as well. I know I did! I felt such rage erupting in me after verbalizing the abuses I'd gone through. None of this had ever been spoken aloud in my family and it was something I'd kept silent and tightly locked up since I was nine years old.

In that moment, everything was bubbling up so I grabbed my pillow and screamed until I was worn out ... and then the tears came. But once this was over I felt lighter than I had in a very long time. That shadow part wasn't erased, but it was releasing and dissolving, slowly but surely.

Learning what your shadow needs to tell you will take conscious effort. Over time you've become deaf and blind to those thoughts and reactions flowing through you. They've become habits. So much so that you probably weren't aware of how much it's controlled your everyday life. It's tough work, but if you want to heal those parts of yourself, it's a must.

Be warned though that your shadow-self isn't going to go along with things easily. It hates change and will fight you every step of the way. Keep vigilant for the tactics it will use to get you to avoid this healing process. Your shadow will do all it can to keep you trapped in that victim mode. After all, it's been replaying the same programs nonstop. It's up to you to take charge and create new life-scripts so you can be your best possible self.

Dissolving Shadow-Projections

Think of someone you absolutely cannot stand. This could be someone you know—a family member, coworker, friend, acquaintance—even a celebrity or public figure. These feelings you have of disgust or anger are all projections of your shadow. These emotion-based judgments are always projections of ourselves and stem from unresolved issues in our past.

Now let's get to work at dissolving this shadow!

1. Get a pen and paper or your journal if you have one and write down the name of the person you're thinking of.

2. List the things about them that make you feel upset, angry, disgusted, envious, or any other negative feeling they arouse in you.

3. Write down the negative things you usually say or think about this person.

Earlier, when I talked about my friend who spends her money on frivolous things I would say things like, "I can't believe how financially irresponsible she is! She's so spoiled and acts so self-entitled. No wonder her finances are a huge wreck and she's declared bankruptcy in the past. Some people never learn the value of money!"

4. Now ask yourself what you do so you can prove to yourself and others that you aren't like this person and write that down.

For me, I would always be very frugal with my money and often deny myself even small pleasures. I rarely bought anything new, instead opting for second-hand items. I would eat the cheapest foods I could make at home and only ate out very occasionally. To me, this proved how financially responsible I was.

5. Look deep inside yourself and ask when you've been just like this person or if someone else when you were younger was like this.

In my case, my parents were terrible with their money. We were always being evicted, seldom had enough food to eat, and would get exactly one new pair of shoes a year. My parents would spend their money on things that brought them only momentary gratification. (With them it was drugs and alcohol.)

So, I learned that spending money on things you don't really need was bad and it became part of my shadow. As I got older this only intensified until I was projecting it outward onto others because I hadn't resolved this issue or even bothered to examine it at all. I just felt like I was naturally wired to be "financially responsible" and had every right to judge others who weren't.

In reality, if I didn't have this issue in the first place, I wouldn't have even noticed that my friend spent her money this way. We can't see in others what doesn't exist within ourselves—good or bad.

As you become more aware of your shadow projections you'll be able to dissolve them over time and can begin to accept them more in others. Once you get to this acceptance stage you'll find that your shadow stops appearing so often.

During the healing process though, know that it's normal to have negative feelings about others. Your shadow is simply showing you where you need to heal and is helping you to learn more about yourself.

Another interesting thing that happens once your shadow starts dissolving is you'll become more aware when you judge others. In reality, this shows that you aren't really judging them at all because you're consciously aware of it. We only judge others, or whatever other shadow projection you've been acting on all these years, when you're unconscious of it. Eventually, you'll heal those old wounds.

Letting Go Of Resistance

If healing our old wounds is so important, why do we ignore it or resist it? Because, we need to make the conscious choice to fully accept all parts of ourselves. Every emotion that's been bottled up inside is valid and every part that feels angry, wounded, guilty, or ashamed is 100% lovable.

Think of it this way, if your best friend or child came to you saying they felt sad or upset what would you say to them? Would you tell them they were being overly dramatic or too sensitive? Would you yell at them, ignore them, or lock them out of the house? No, you wouldn't. And yet, this is exactly what we do to our child selves.

Imagine that much younger you standing outside in the dark, banging on the door, trying desperately to get your attention and your help. But you've closed the curtains, put in earplugs, and distracted yourself from paying attention. Doesn't that sound heartbreaking?

It's time to open that door and embrace your shadow. Shine light on it, get into those dark corners, listen, and pay attention to what it needs. Once you do, this inner self that you once felt so separated from will integrate with you and transform.

Yes, your shadow will always be part of you. Although I talk about "dissolving" your shadow, it's really more like integrating with it. Why? Because you can't erase the past. But, you'll find that with acceptance your shadow ends up being far more helpful.

One of the most difficult things though is getting over our resistance to acknowledging and working with this shadow. Here are some ways to work through this.

1. Allow yourself to truly experience any emotion that comes up for you. We get so used to being distracted, ignoring, or denying our emotions that we aren't really living or working through anything.

This goes for even the good things you experience. It's far too easy to live superficially these days. When you feel something, really feel it. Pay attention to what it's telling you or just immerse yourself in the sensations.

When my grandmother died I pushed that pain down for a long, long time. I felt it though. That tightness in my chest. That lump in my throat and the burning in my eyes. It just hurt too bad to dive into this and experience all I truly felt, so I ignored it. Soon, all those emotions started turning into anger and I knew that wasn't good.

One day I was looking at a magazine and saw a grandmotherly-type woman on the cover. Suddenly, I heard this voice in my head say, "Why is she still alive and my grandma is dead!" I felt so much rage, but I let it flow through me. Soon, the rage turned into grief and I cried ... a lot. Luckily I was at home when this happened because that part of my shadow had gotten a lot bigger and stronger over time.

And then that piece of myself started healing. It was such a huge release and afterward, although I still missed her, all of that sorrow and anger was gone. Instead, good and funny memories of the past filled that dark place inside me.

Don't deny your emotions. Experience them. Feel them to the fullest. Then let it go.

2. Keep reminding yourself that there's nothing wrong or unacceptable with any part of you. The problem is, your mind loves to judge, and your mind was programmed long ago by the adults and experiences in your life. You're expected to act this way, do this thing, don't do that, don't say this, and be sure you do what's acceptable.

All of these negative messages just pile up over time, making you feel there's something wrong with you. You're somehow not good enough unless you act a certain way. Do yourself a favor and disconnect from all of that. Acknowledge what this wounded part of you is saying and send it love.

3. When you go through the process of emotional healing and releasing all of those old, outworn programs you'll probably have times where you feel a lot of discomfort or detachment. You might not consciously notice it, but some telltale signs that you need to ground yourself and stop avoiding the healing process are:

- Eating when you aren't hungry

- Excessively watching TV or playing video games

- Browsing the internet for long periods

- Taking naps every day, even if you got enough sleep the night before

- Anything that has you avoiding dealing with what's coming up inside you

Reconnecting your mind, body, and spirit is important during the healing process. Simple things like taking walks outside, being in nature, gardening, dancing, breathing exercises, meditation, yoga, tai chi, and other gentle exercises can help ground you as you work through this healing.

4. Self-care and self-nurturing is a must at any time, but especially when doing shadow work. You need to do things that bring you a sense of calm and release. Pursue your favorite creative outlets whether music, art, dance, nature, or anything else that brings you comfort. Take a hot bath, meditate while listening to soothing music, read books that lift you up and excite you, cook delicious yet nutritious meals, and get emotional support from people who care about you.

Shadows In Your Relationships

Without thought, we're constantly projecting onto others what we don't want to face or accept within ourselves. We do it so these issues or behaviors remain out of sight to everyone around us. If we ignore these things we can act like they don't exist, but this doesn't work. Instead, all of those repressed feelings of anger, hurt, or shame become stronger and our shadow grows bigger and darker.

But, it can't stay hidden forever. So, all of this gets projected onto your partner and we judge them, blame them, and disapprove of them and their actions. It's like they're living under a microscope and we see every perceived flaw, every little thing that annoys us about them. We see all of their shortcomings and faults.

Think of your current relationship if you're in one, or a past relationship. What about this person did you detest? What did they do that grated on your nerves? Those very things are right there inside your shadow and you've been trying to hide them.

Since relationships are a mirror of our deepest selves, it won't stay buried for long. If you want to heal your current relationship or find a more stable and fulfilling one you're going to need to do some shadow work.

Relationship Shadow Work Exercise:

1. Get a pen and paper or your journal and write down all the things that you don't/didn't like about your partner. Was this

person lazy? Greedy? A know-it-all? A chronic complainer? Get it all out, every single trait you couldn't stand.

2. For each negative trait you wrote down, think about (then write down) times when you've displayed this type of behavior. Even if we don't want to admit it, we all have at one time or another. Or, was there someone from your childhood who acted this way and so you've learned that these traits are negative and you've done your best to never be like this person?

These two steps seem deceptively simple, but facing your own darker side takes a lot of courage. When you see the truth written in your own words it's hard to ignore or deny it. This type of shadow work is really helpful in resolving relationship conflicts because we can see how like attracts like. You gravitated toward this person so you can work on your own stuff. And, they gravitated toward you for the same purpose.

Ideally, you should be able to work with your partner on your individual and combined issues following the other exercises in this book. However, a lot of times shadow work is a solitary road. Not everyone is brave enough and open to resolving conflicts and facing their shadow self. That's okay though. You need to focus on yourself and your own healing. Trust that your relationship(s) will heal or fall away as needed for your highest good.

Don't be disappointed if things don't resolve themselves right away. It's going to take time and effort to work through these shadow parts of yourself. They've been living and growing inside you for many, many years, but by acknowledging them and finding the root cause of them (usually from childhood traumas) you'll be able to stop projecting those repressed issues onto your partner.

Eventually, your shadow projections will naturally dissolve and your relationship with your partner will be so much happier and healthier. If you aren't currently in a relationship, you'll be able to attract a partner who's a mirror of your lighter side rather than your darker side.

Sorting Through Your Stuff

One of the things I've noticed over the decades of doing psychic counseling is how many people, including myself in the past, believe that other people make us happy or make us miserable. Honestly, only you can do both. As a child, you didn't have a choice or a voice. As an adult though, you're the one in charge of your ultimate happiness or misery.

I like this quote, often ascribed to Eleanor Roosevelt, "No one can make you feel inferior without your consent." That's actually very true. Nobody can cast a spell over you to *make* you feel hurt.

The reason you feel hurt is because that wounded part of yourself is telling you that what this person said or did is the truth and we're wrong to think otherwise. (It's not true, but it's what we believe.) We also hurt ourselves when something or someone in our life doesn't meet up with our expectations of how we think it should be. But we stick this hurt down in the basement of our minds and leave it there, never realizing that this shadow will continually be fed, growing bigger and bigger, until we're forced to deal with it.

The way I imagine my shadow looking at times is a hoarder's home. Massive amounts of "stuff" everywhere. The mess is so overwhelming you have no idea where to even start cleaning it up, so it's easier just to ignore it.

That is, until it starts crowding you out and you have no other choice but to start working on those massive piles. But, it's not as easy as just tossing it all out. Instead, each piece of this hoard has to be examined first so you know what to do with it.

Examining Your Hoard:

I always suggest keeping notes, thoughts, and exercises in a journal. This way you can go back over it again in the future and see how much you've grown and changed, and where more healing needs to take place. Write down your responses to the following:

- This is what my shadow self does

- This is why I do it

- This is how this shadow affects me

- This is how it affects those around me

- This is how I can change it and heal

Using myself as an example, I've responded this way:

When nobody helps me with chores around the house I feel taken advantage of and disrespected. Instead of talking to people and asking for help, I become silent and passive-aggressive.

I do it because while growing up my parents never let me have a voice or opinions. I was also expected to do most of the household chores myself, though I always felt it was unfair.

This part of my shadow impacts me because I close myself off from the people I love and I feel distant from them. It also makes me feel guilty and embarrassed for acting like this when there are better ways to handle it.

It impacts those around me because they know something is off about me. I appear stressed and distant. But, since I never ask for help, they believe that "Mom loves cleaning!" and I'm just in the cleaning zone. To them, it's the norm.

The way to change this and heal is to simply open my mouth and ask for help. I don't have to be rude or huff around while I do it all myself. I can simply say, "Hey, I'll do the dishes if you take out the trash" or something like this. That way they're aware that I want help and know what I expect of them and I won't feel so overwhelmed or irritated.

Do this exercise for each and every one of your shadows. You don't need to do it all in one sitting. In fact, you probably couldn't even if you tried. There's a lot in there that needs to be examined and worked through. I've been doing shadow work for several years now and I'm always discovering something new about myself.

Releasing Shadows Of The Past

Clients have often asked me why it's so easy to forget or let go of the good things we experience, yet we hold on and rehash our bad experiences again and again. Because, you haven't processed the negative experiences yet. It's easy to process the good stuff because it feels positive, light, and happy. So we don't hold on to it long. Negative things though? They seem to take up residence in our soul and color our world.

And, the longer we carry these around—whether consciously or unconsciously—they have more effect on our lives. Not only will these shadows have control of your mind, but they'll eventually take over your physical body as well. Many illnesses that doctors can find no cause of—various aches and pains, chronic fatigue, mysterious allergies, and more—often stem from repressed emotions.

Clearing the shadows of the past isn't easy, but absolutely necessary if you want to live a life of abundance. So often though we're unaware that our shadow self is running and ruining our lives. It's been with you for so long it just seems like "the way things are". Something bad happens and you push it aside or act like it's no big deal. But it *is* a big deal and if you don't process it once and for all it will continue to be the driving force in your life.

We've all had trauma and drama in our lives that created these shadows. Since we're near the end of the book, you already know this. You've also come to learn that if you don't start clearing them out you'll just add to your current collection of shadows. As the years go by, the mental, emotional, and physical toll all of this takes on you will simply grow.

If you're honest with yourself, you'll see that denying your shadow, shoving it aside, squashing it down, or completely ignoring it hasn't worked. If anything, it's gotten stronger and has guided your life far more than you want to admit to.

Sometimes, I'm shocked when I realize what event caused which part of my shadow. When I was in third grade I remember trying out to be a dancer in a school performance. I practiced and practiced. The day came to try out, I did my best, and didn't make it. I ended up being in the very back of the chorus instead. I was heartbroken, angry, and couldn't understand why, after working so hard, I was rejected. And that was the lesson I learned that day, "It doesn't matter how hard you try, it won't be good enough."

For some people, this might have turned into a lifetime of never really trying at all. For me, I tried harder, became a perfectionist, and my own worst critic. Sure, there were other things that happened before and after that contributed to this "rejection-shadow", but not getting a part in the dance wasn't something I thought about much after it was over. Only when I was doing my own shadow work did it rise up to the surface.

And that's how shadow work is. Rather than just one shadow that came into being from one huge trauma in your past, it's made up of many, many small and large experiences. Think of your shadow as a huge jigsaw puzzle. Each time you find a piece of it you examine it and replace that dark piece with a light piece. You might have thousands of puzzle pieces inside you. Some relate to shame, or guilt, or anger, or sadness, and so forth.

Even if you find the first root cause of one of your issues, it's not going to fade away in the blink of an eye. I learned that lesson one day when I admitted to myself during the mirror-work exercise how my step-father sexually abused me. This instilled feelings of shame, fear, and even anger within me. Okay, I admitted it, I allowed those feelings to come to the surface, problem solved, right? Nope. Not by a long shot.

Because of the initial abuse, over the years I ended up experiencing other forms of shame, fear, and anger. And they all got stuffed into my shadow and became more pieces of that puzzle. I had to work through each one, and I'm still finding more. Over time though I've felt a loosening up inside me, a dissolving of those dark, tight emotions. Those shadow ripples that used to touch upon so many areas of my life are now receding more and more each day.

While doing shadow work, never be afraid of what you'll find. There's nothing horrible or scary inside of you. Instead, it's about taking responsibility and finding the wisdom in those darker areas, then making it part of your conscious world. Once this happens your shadow side will no longer control you or your life. You'll finally be the one in charge, making much better decisions about your finances, relationships, your health, and everything you do.

Contact Me/Book A Reading

Whether your problems or concerns are in the areas of love, finances, family, career, health, education, or your path in life, I offer professional psychic counseling, caring guidance, and solutions that work!

I use no tools. Instead, I'll connect directly with your higher self and your spirit guides to help you through any situation and achieve the best possible results. No problem is too big or too small, and your questions will be answered in detail.

I'll let you know absolutely everything that comes through in the reading which typically includes past, present, and future energies, guidance, time frames and predictions. Your guides may also include information on an important past life, aura energy, soul symbols, and more. Each reading is in-depth, filled with positive energy and guidance, and includes one free clarification email.

All readings are done via email. By offering my readings through email you'll be able to save your reading and go back to it again and again for guidance.

I look forward to reading for you!

Check out my readings, books, blog posts, and more on my website:

DrKellyPsychic.com

1. http://psychicreadingsbydrkelly.webs.com/psychic-readings

CPSIA information can be obtained
at www.ICGtesting.com
Printed in the USA
BVHW031951200222
629605BV00018B/194

9 781393 116707